Four Sisters

Harlan R. Musil

NEWMAN SPRINGS PUBLISHING
320 Broad Street
Red Bank, NJ 07701

First originally published by Newman Springs Publishing 2023

ISBN 979-8-88763-819-5 (Paperback)
ISBN 979-8-89061-414-8 (Hardcover)
ISBN 979-8-88763-820-1 (Digital)

Printed in the United States of America

I would like to dedicate this book to my partner, Jamus Mudloff, and to Fatima Al-Jibory, who both inspired me in writing this book.

Four sisters, different in so many ways.

Each unique in how they spend their days.

At first glance, you might think they all are the same.

With only the difference between them being their name.

Similar height, weight, body type, hair, and eye color too.

How can anyone tell them apart from who is who?

Fatima, the oldest, is kind, witty, and smart.

She works with special-needs kids and has a kind heart.

The second-oldest sister, Zahraa, is outgoing and fun.

If you play laser tag with her, you better run.

The third-born, Zanib, is the most reserved and quiet by far.

To be clear, she even has the word *antisocial* on her car.

The youngest, Hawra, is a talented artist, you see.

She writes, paints, draws, and tattoos, making it look so easy.

The two middle sisters work in a pharmacy.

They help take care of everyone's sick family.

The youngest sister is a cashier right now.

But she wants to be a successful artist...wow!

All four sisters go to the gym to workout.

Fatima goes most days while the others hang about.

The sisters all love to listen to music in their car.

Hawra is the only sister who goes to concerts so far.

5

All the sisters like to work on their automobiles.

They have a passion for cars and how it makes them feel.

Fatima, Zahraa, Zanib, and Hawra drive their cars really fast.

Like most Americans, they only slow down to save on gas.

Hawra
Zanib
Zahraa
Fatima

Football, basketball, tennis, golf,
boxing, soccer, and bowling too.

These are just a few of the sports
the sisters like to do.

All four sisters were raised
in the USA from birth.

Each following the American dream
and proving their worth.

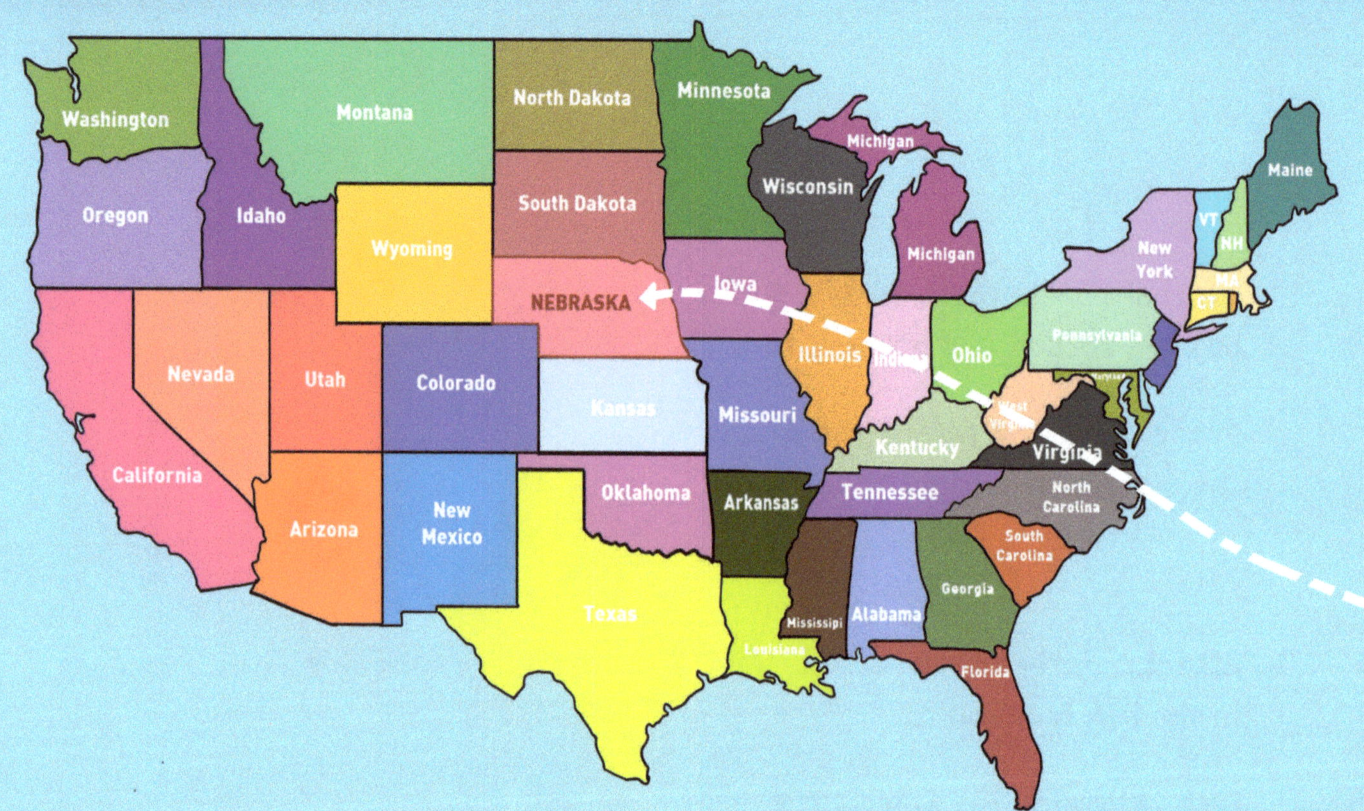

Their parents immigrated from Iraq and follow the Islamic religion.

Like most Buddhists, Christians, Hindus and Jews, were born into it and not their decision.

Russia
Kazakhstan
Uzbekistan
Turkmenistan
Turkey
Greece
Syria
IRAQ
Iran
Egypt
Saudi
Arabia
UAE
Oman
Sudan
Yemen

ISLAM IS THE BELIEF
Fatima
Zahraa
Zanib
Hawra

Islam is their belief and, just like other religions,
has different branches or sectors.

Similar to the Christian faith having Baptists,
Catholics, Lutheran, Methodist and others.

Muslims may pray three or five times every day.

Who are we to say how they should or should not pray.

Many Muslims have their own prayer mat.

They may carry it with them,
so they can pray anywhere in fact.

Islam
Judaism
Buddhism
Christianity
Hinduism
Native American
Wicca

There are many different religious and agnostic beliefs
in the USA, it's true.

Buddhism, Christianity, Hinduism, Islam, Judaism,
Native American, Wicca and atheism, to name a few.

Muslim women wear head scarves called hijab or *Khimar*.

Their culture and beliefs are not better or worse.
It's simply a part of who they are.

RAMADAN

SUHUR

5-7 AM

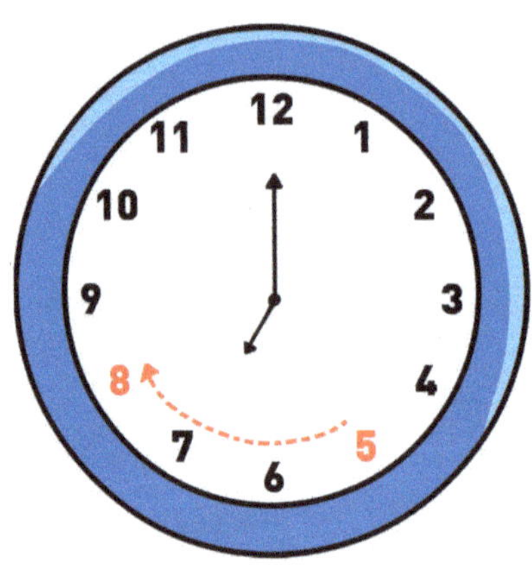

5 AM & 8 PM

6-8 PM

IFTAR

FAST
DON'T EAT
OR
DRINK

Muslims celebrate Ramadan for a whole month each year.

They go without food and water from sunrise to sunset,
my dear.

The traditional foods of the Islamic faith,

May at first not look or sound too great.

During Ramadan, they rise before dawn to eat *suhur*
(*soo-her*).

Foods with grains, seeds, dates, and bananas they prefer.

At sunset, the fast is broken with iftar,
a meal that starts usually with dates.

The rest of the meal might include assorted meze
(appetizers), and it all tastes great.

NOT PORK

Wheat, barley, rice, and dates are staple foods in Iraq.

They also eat camel, chicken, cow, fish, goat, lamb, sheep and Yak.

Masgouf, *pacha*, and *torshi* are three native Iraq cuisines.

Eating hamburgers, fries, and pizza is also in
the sisters' routine.

The sisters all eat a variety of American foods.

Their heritage, although different, they eat
the same as me and you.

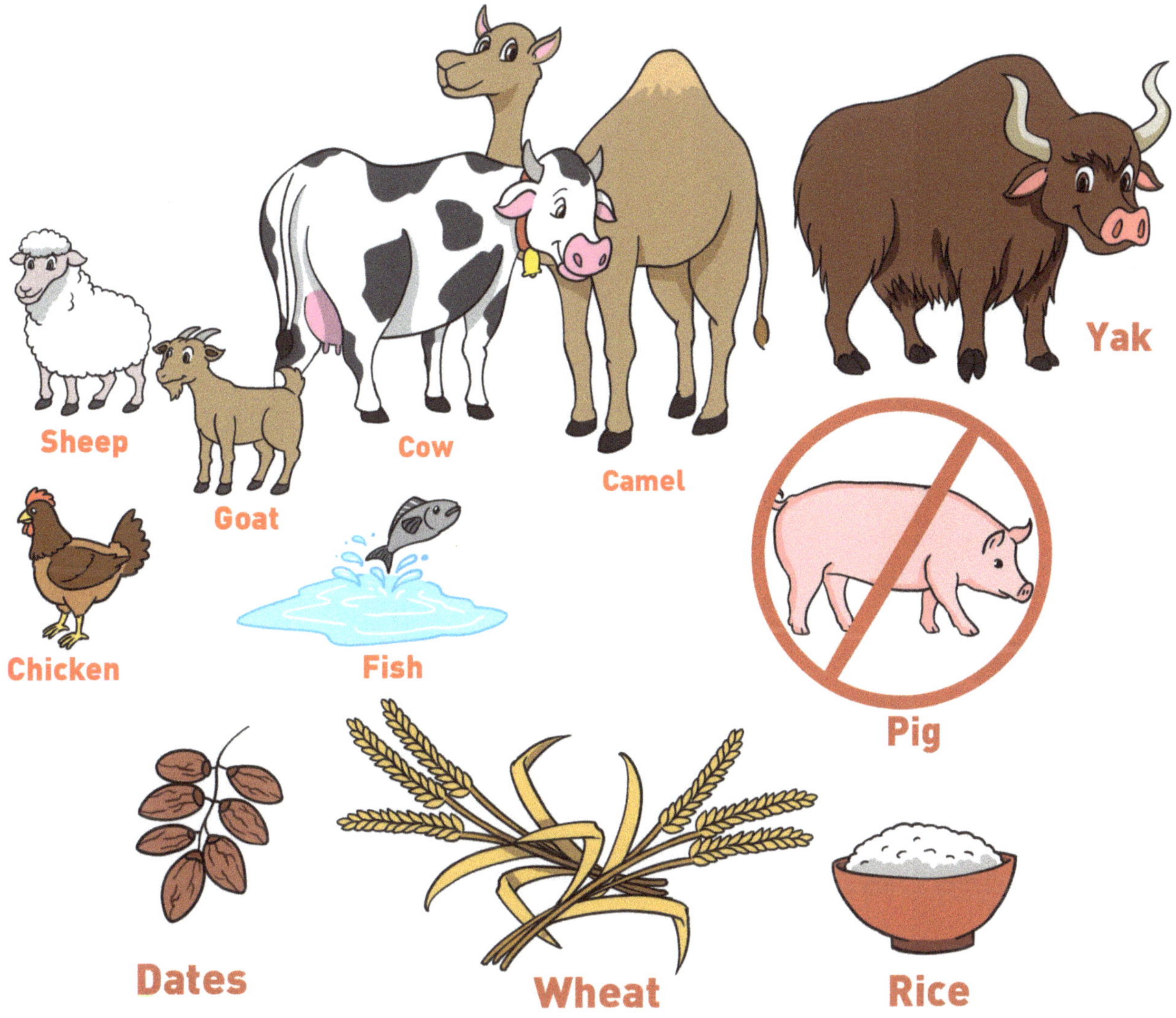
Sheep
Goat
Cow
Camel
Yak
Chicken
Fish
Pig
Dates
Wheat
Rice

Zanib
Fatima
Zahraa
Hawra
ZANIB
FATIMA
ZAHRAA
HAWRA

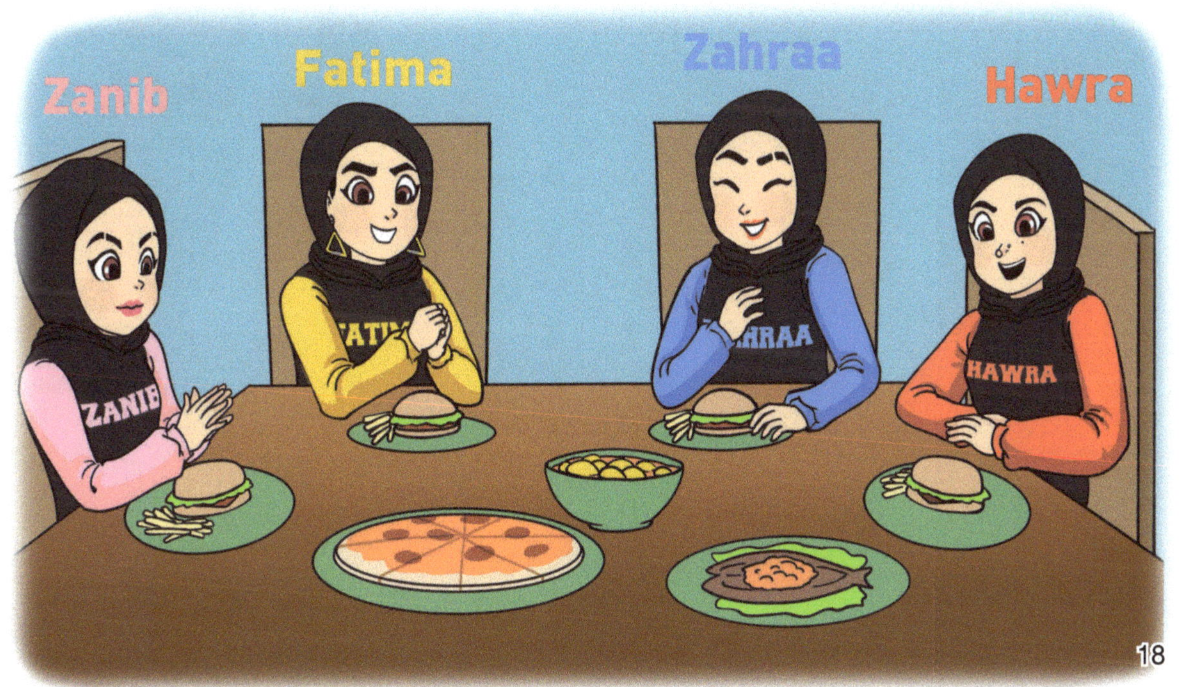

Four American sisters so diverse and similar to other Americans today.

All celebrate their cultural diversity and the American way.

The sisters have four brothers, that's another story.

There will likely be a second book, so don't you worry.

Washington
Montana
North Dakota
Minnesota
Oregon
Idaho
Wyoming
South Dakota
Wisconsin
Michigan
Michigan
Maine
VT
NH
New York
Nevada
Utah
Colorado
NEBRASKA
Iowa
Illinois
Indiana
Ohio
Pennsylvania
CT
California
Kansas
Missouri
West Virginia
Virginia
Kentucky
North Carolina
Arizona
New Mexico
Oklahoma
Arkansas
Tennessee
South Carolina
Texas
Mississipi
Alabama
Georgia
Louisiana
Florida

Zahraa

ZANIB
FATIMA
HAWRA

Four sisters born in America who are Muslim they say.

It's who they are and no different from other Americans in the USA.

The end.

Resource Information

Masgouf is a whole-skewered fish barbecued on an outdoor grill.

Pacha is a slowly cooked combination of sheep's head, stomach, feet, and other parts in a broth.

Torshi is a mixture of pickled vegetables.

Meze refers to appetizers such as assorted nuts, fava beans, lentil soup, bread, and fresh fruit eaten at Iftar.

Iftar is the evening meal (of dates) that breaks each day's fast during Ramadan.

The astrolabe is an ancient astronomical instrument that allows the user to calculate astronomical positions precisely. There is also a prayer line which guides when it's time to pray.

The exact and precise time to pray is very important in Islam and shows strength in their faith.

The astrolabe is used to determine the prayer direction they face called qiblah. Muslims pray to face the sacred mosque located in Mecca (Makkah). Today qiblah can be found using modern geographic location technology.

A prayer mat is called different names by different sectors of the Islamic religion.

The Quran, also Romanized Qur'an or Koran, is the central religious text of Islam, believed by Muslims to be the revelation from God.

Muslims worship in temples called mosques.

Mosques are built with qiblah positioning to have the front of the building facing the city of Mecca.

Qiblah is the direction the Muslims are to face that points to the sacred city of Mecca.

Islam is the name of the religion.

Muslim is the faith identification of the people.

Middle Easterners can be of other faiths such as Christian or Jewish.

In 2023, there are over eight billion people in the world with two billion being Islam/Muslims.

In the USA, there are 335 million people with 3.4 million being Muslim.

Muslims are followers of the Islamic faith. Islam is an Abrahamic, monotheistic religion that began in the seventh century AD, although its roots are believed to date back further. Islam was created in the city of Mecca, located in modern-day Saudi Arabia. Most Muslims live in North and Central Africa, the Middle East, and Southeast Asia.

Islam Is the World's Second-Largest Religion

Earth is home to more than 1.9 billion Muslims. Islam is also the world's fastest-growing religion. The Islamic population is mainly split between 1.5 billion Sunni Muslims and 240 to 340 million Shia Muslims, with the remainder scattered among a few smaller denominations.

A Muslim-majority country is one in which more than 50 percent of the people are Muslims. There are currently approximately fifty Muslim-majority countries in the world, although the precise number differs slightly depending on the source. In most cases, these inconsistencies can be attributed to one of two causes. First is the age of the estimate, which is relevant because the Muslim population in each country tends to grow, raising the nationwide percentage of Muslims over time. The second cause is that some sources include various regions such as Western Sahara or Palestine, which are sometimes considered countries and sometimes considered territories, and other sources do not.

The Pew Research Center acknowledged a total of fifty Muslim-majority nations (including territories of West Bank, Gaza Strip, Mayotte, and Western Sahara) in the world in 2010 but added Nigeria to its 2020 estimate to reach fifty-one. In comparison, the *2021 United States CIA World Factbook* leaves out the territories Mayotte and Western Sahara—and somewhat inexplicably, the country of Kazakhstan—but adds Bosnia and Herzegovina for a total of forty-nine.

Another country that is currently left off of most lists of Muslim-majority countries but which may be added someday soon is Eritrea, whose Muslim population has been estimated to be as low as 36.6 percent and as high as

51.6 percent. If updated numbers become available, Eritrea may well become the newest Muslim-majority country.

Top ten countries with the highest percentage of Muslims in 2021:

1. Maldives—100 percent
2. Mauritania—99.9 percent
3. Somalia—99.8 percent (tie)
4. Tunisia—99.8 percent (tie)
5. Afghanistan—99.7 percent (tie)
6. Algeria—99.7 percent (tie)
7. Iran—99.4 percent
8. Yemen—99.2 percent
9. Morocco—99 percent
10. Niger—98.3 percent

Note: At 99.4 percent Muslim, the disputed territory Western Sahara would rank at number 8, but as it has not yet been recognized as a country by the United Nations, it was disqualified.

Although the countries listed above have the highest concentrations of Muslim citizens, it's worth noting that many larger countries have more Muslims overall.

Top ten countries with the most Muslims in 2021:

1. Indonesia—231,000,000
2. Pakistan—212,300,000
3. India—200,000,000
4. Bangladesh—153,700,000
5. Nigeria—95,000,000-103,000,000
6. Egypt—85,000,000-90,000,000
7. Iran—82,500,000

8. Turkey—74,432,725
9. Algeria—41,240,913
10. Sudan—39,585,777

The Quran and Fundamentals of Islam

Muslims worship the same God, whom they typically refer to as Allah, as do Christians, Jews, and the Bahá'í faith. While Muslims acknowledge that spiritual figures such as Adam, Moses, and Jesus were prophets, they believe the prophet Muhammad was sent to convey Allah's final teachings.

These teachings are contained in the Quran (often spelled *Qur'an* or *Koran*), Islam's religious text, which Muslims believe to be God's verbatim words, which were revealed to Muhammad. Muslims also follow a legal system known as Sharia law, a faith-based code of conduct that includes guidelines for nearly every aspect of Muslim life.

Muslims follow five fundamental pillars that are essential to their faith. These are known as the five pillars of Islam.

The five pillars of Islam:

- Shahada: One must recite the shahada, declaring one's faith in God and belief in Muhammad.
- Salat: One must pray five times per day: at dawn, noon, afternoon, sunset, and evening, while facing toward the Ka'bah, a mosque in Mecca.
- Zakat: One must give to those in need.
- Sawm: One must fast from dawn to sunset during Ramadan.
- Hajj: One must make a pilgrimage to Mecca at least once during a person's lifetime if possible.

Sources

1. Pew Research Center, "Muslim-Majority Countries."
2. CIA World Factbook, "Field Listing: Religions."
3. Pew Research Center, "Religious Composition by Country, 2010–2050."

About the Author

Harlan R. Musil is a Nebraska native, born in Grand Island, Nebraska. He was raised in Columbus, Nebraska, and currently lives in Lincoln, Nebraska, with his partner, Jamus. He studied at the University of Nebraska-Lincoln and has a bachelor of science in home economics with a focus on nutrition and dietetics and a master's in food service management with a focus on food service design. Harlan served in the US Army and has worked in many food service environments, including fast food, fine dining, hospital, day care, assisted living, and nursing home operations.

Harlan has been involved in supporting community diversity throughout the majority of his life. Harlan also worked in Nebraska corrections and at the University of Nebraska housing as a production manager. Harlan taught culinary at Southeast Community College and was an adjunct instructor at the University of Nebraska-Lincoln. He has owned and operated a gay nightclub called the Q and Libations, a Cigar Martini Bar and Reception Hall. Harlan's contact with a very diverse population has helped him better understand the struggles of minority groups such as the LGBTQIA+, African American, Asian, Middle Eastern, Native American, religious affiliation, gender, VETs, elderly, mentally challenged, disabled, incarcerated, homeless, working poor, immigrants, and DACA recipients. Harlan has a drive to problem-solve and make things better. His personal belief is that everyone has value and is important with something to offer.

9 7 9 8 8 8 7 6 3 8 1 9 5